George Washington, A. (Albert) Jackson

Authenticated Copy of the Last Will and Testament of

George Washington

George Washington, A. (Albert) Jackson

Authenticated Copy of the Last Will and Testament of George Washington

ISBN/EAN: 9783337010003

Printed in Europe, USA, Canada, Australia, Japan

Cover: Foto ©ninafisch / pixelio.de

More available books at **www.hansebooks.com**

AUTHENTICATED COPY

OF THE

LAST WILL AND TESTAMENT

OF

GEORGE WASHINGTON,

OF MT. VERNON,

EMBRACING A SCHEDULE OF HIS REAL ESTATE
AND NOTES THERETO BY THE TESTATOR.

TO WHICH IS ADDED
HISTORICAL NOTES AND BIOGRAPHICAL SKETCHES,
BY THE PUBLISHER.

A. JACKSON, Publisher,
Washington, D. C.
1868.
Sam'l Polkinhorn, Printer.

EXITUS ACTA PROBAT

G. Washington

TO

W. W. CORCORAN, Esq.;

OF

WASHINGTON, D. C.

This Volume is respectfully Dedicated by the

PUBLISHER.

01084 8306

STATE OF VIRGINIA, } To Wit:
FAIRFAX COUNTY,

I Ferdinand D Richardson
Clerk of the County Court of said County,
do hereby Certify that, this Copy of the
Last Will and Testament of General
George Washington with the Schedule
and his notes thereto attached, has
been carefully examined and compared
with the Original now on file in my
Office among the Records of the said
Court, and further, that, I find the
same to be in all respects a correct
copy of the same.

In Testimony whereof
I have hereunto subscribed
my name and affixed the
seal of the said Court this
14 day of April A D 1868,
and in the 92 year of the
Commonwealth.

F. D. RICHARDSON c c

PREFACE.

The last Will and Testament of Washington, never before published entire, is contained in this volume. It would be useless to enter into an explanation of the motives which have induced its publication—but it may be remarked that the design was conceived during the late war, and was suggested by the declaration in the public journals, oft repeated and seldom contradicted that, "the will had been abstracted from the clerks office of Fairfax County Court, by the Rebel clerk, sold and was on exhibition in the British museum." A recent perusal, inspection and facilities for copying the same, have enabled the publisher to reproduce it here. The mutilated condition of the manuscript from frequent handling, rendered it impracticable to take a lithographic copy; but the pages given in this volume present the same number of lines to the page, the same words upon each line, and the same quaint orthography as the original, and at the bottom of each page a *fac simile* of the signature of the Testator as it appears in the manuscript Will.

Apart from the interest which must attach to the will of Washington as a portion of his private history, the reader will not fail to remark its appropriate teachings in regard to the great social and political problem which is yet but half solved, and which for years to come, will continue to tax the sagacity, the forbearance, and the patriotism of the whole people.

FAIRFAX C. H., VA., *May,* 1868.

THE PUBLISHER.

In the name of God, Amen!

I George Washington[1] of Mount
Vernon,[2] a citizen of the United States
and lately President of the same
do make ordain and declare this
Instrument, which is written with
my own hand and every page[3] there-
-of subscribed with my name to be
my last Will & Testament,[4] revo-
-king all others.

—*Imprimus*—All my debts, of which there
are but few, and none of magnitude,
are to be punctually and speedily paid,
and the legacies hereinafter bequeathed
are to be discharged as soon as cir-
-cumstances will permit, and in the
manner directed.

Item—To my dearly beloved wife, Mar-
-tha Washington[5] I give and bequeath
the use profit and benefit of my whole
Estate, real and personal, for the term
of her natural life, except such parts
thereof as are specially disposed
of hereafter,—My improved lot in
the Town of Alexandria, situated on
Pitt and Cameron Streets, I give to her &
her heirs forever, as I also do my

household and kitchen furniture of
every sort and kind with the liquors and
groceries which may be on hand at
the time of my decease, to be used and
disposed of as she may think proper

ITEM—Upon the decease of my wife it is
my will and desire, that all the slaves
which I hold in *my own right* shall
receive their freedom[6]—To emanci-
-pate them during her life, would tho
earnestly wished by me, be attended
with such insuperable difficulties, on
account of their intermixture by mar-
-riages with the Dower negroes[7] as to
excite the most painful sensations,—
if not disagreeable consequences from
the latter while both descriptions are
in the occupancy of the same propri-
-etor, it not being in my power under
the tenure by which the dower Negroes
are held to manumit them——And
whereas among those who will re-
-ceive freedom according to this de-
-vise there may be some who from
old age, or bodily infirmities & others
who on account of their infancy, that
will be unable to support themselves,[8]
it is my will and desire that all who
come under the first and second descrip-
-tion shall be comfortably clothed and
fed by my heirs while they live and

that such of the latter description as
have no parents living, or if living
are unable, or unwilling to provide
for them, shall be bound by the Court
until they shall arrive at the age of
twenty five years, and in cases where
no record can be produced whereby
their ages can be ascertained, the Judg-
-ment of the Court upon it's own view
of the subject shall be adequate and
final.——The negroes thus bound are
(by their masters or mistresses) to be
taught to read and write[9] and to be brought
up to some useful occupation, agree-
-ably to the laws of the Commonwealth
of Virginia, providing for the support
of orphans and other poor children
—and I do hereby expressly forbid
the sale or transportation out of the
said Commonwealth of any Slave I may
die possessed *of*, under any pretence
whatsoever—and I do moreover
most positively, and most solemnly
enjoin it upon my Executors hereafter
named, or the survivors of them
to see that *this* clause respecting slaves
and every part thereof be religious-
-ly fulfilled at the Epoch at which it
is directed to take place without evasion
neglect or delay after the crops
which may then may be on the ground are
harvested, particularly as it respects—

the aged and infirm, seeing that a regular and permanent fund be established
for their support so long as there are
subjects requiring it, not trusting to
the uncertain provisions to be made by
individuals.——And to my mulatto
man, William (calling himself William
Lee[10]) I give immediate freedom or if
he should prefer it (on account of the
accidents which have befallen him and
which have rendered him incapable of
walking or of any active employment)
to remain in the situation he now is,
it shall be optional in him to do so—In
either case however I allow him an
annuity of thirty dollars during his
natural life which shall be indepen-
-dent of the victuals and *cloaths* he has
been accustomed to receive; if he *chuses*
the last alternative, but in full with
his freedom, if he prefers the first, and this
I give him as a testimony of my sense
of his attachment to me and for his
faithful services during the revolutionary
War.

ITEM—To the Trustees, (Governors or by whatsoever other name they may be designated)
of the Academy in the Town of Alexan-
-dria,[11] I give and bequeath, in Trust,
Four thousand dollars, or in other
words twenty of the shares which I

hold in the Bank of Alexandria to-
-wards the support of a Free School, es-
-tablished at, and annexed to the said Acad-
-emy for the purpose of educating such
orphan children, or the children of such
other poor and indigent persons as are
unable to accomplish it with their own
means, and who in the judgment of
the trustees of the said Seminary, are
best entitled to the benefit of this donation——
The aforesaid twenty shares
I give and bequeath in perpetuity—the
dividends only of which are to be drawn
for and applied by the said Trustees
for the time being, for the uses above
mentioned, the stock to remain entire
and untouched unless indications of
a failure of the said Bank should be
so apparent or discontinuance thereof
should render a removal of this fund
necessary, in either of these cases the
amount of the stock here devised is to
be vested in some other bank or public
institution whereby the interest
may with regularity and certainty be
drawn and applied as above.——And
to prevent misconception, my mean-
-ing is, and is hereby declared to be that,
these twenty shares are in lieu of and
not in addition to the Thousand pounds
given by a missive letter some years ago
in consequence whereof an an-

-nuity of fifty pounds has since been
paid toward the support of this institution

ITEM—Whereas by a law of the Commonwealth
of Virginia, enacted in the year
1785, the Legislature thereof was
pleased (as an evidence of it's
approbation of the services I
had rendered the public during the
Revolution—and partly, I believe in
consideration of my having suggested
the vast advantages which the com-
-munity would derive from the exten-
-sion of its Inland navigation, under
Legislative patronage) to present me with
one hundred shares, of one hundred dollars
each, in the incorporated company
established for the purpose of exten-
-ding the navigation of James River
from tide water to the mountains;
and also with fifty shares of one
hundred pounds sterling each in the
corporation of another company like-
-wise established for the similar pur-
-pose of opening the navigation of the
River Potomac from tide water to
Fort Cumberland;[12] the acceptance
of which, although the offer was high-
-ly honorable and grateful to my
feelings, was refused, as inconsistent
with a principle which I had adop-

-ted, and had never departed from, namely
not to receive pecuniary compensation
for any services I could render
my country in it's arduous strug-
-gle with Great Britain for it's Rights;
and because I had evaded similar prop-
-ositions from other States in the Union
—adding to this refusal however an
intimation, that, if it should be the
pleasure of the Legislature to permit me to
appropriate the said shares to *public
uses*, I would receive them on those terms
with due sensibility—and this it having
consented to in flatering terms,
as will appear by a subsequent law
and sundry resolutions, in the most
ample and honorable manner, I
proceed after this recital for the
more correct understanding of the
case to declare—

      That as it has always been
a source of serious regret with me
to see the youth of these United States
sent to foreign countries for the pur-
-pose of education, often before their
minds were formed or they had im-
-bibed any adequate ideas of the hap-
-piness of their own, contracting too
frequently not only habits of dissipa-
-tion and *extravagence*, but principles
unfriendly to Republican *Governm't*
and to the true and genuine liberties

of mankind, which thereafter are
rarely overcome.——For these reasons
it has been my ardent wish to
see a plan devised on a liberal scale
which would have a tendency to spread
systamatic ideas through all parts
of this rising Empire, thereby to do
away local attachments and State
prejudices as far as the nature of
things would, or indeed ought to ad·
-mit, from our national councils—
—Looking anxiously forward
to the accomplisment of so desira-
-ble an object as this is, (in my esti-
-mation) my mind has not been able to
contemplate any plan more likely
to effect the measure than the estab-
-lishment of a University in
a central part of the United States
to which the youth of fortune and
talents from all parts thereof might
be sent for the completion of their
education in all the branches of
polite literature in arts and sciences
—in acquiring knowledge in the prin-
-ciples of Politics and good Goverment
—and (as a matter of infinite impor-
-portance in my judgment) by associ-
-ating with each other and forming friend-
-ships in Juvenile years, be enabled
to free themselves in a proper degree
from those local prejudices and habit-

-ual jealousies which have just been
mentioned and which when carried to
excess are never failing sources of
disquietude to the Public mind and
pregnant of mischievous consequen-
-ces to this country:—Under these
impressions so fully dilated,—

ITEM—I give and bequeath in per-
-petuity the fifty shares which I hold
in the Potomac Company (under the
aforesaid Acts of the Legislature of Vir-
-ginia) towards the endowment
of a University[13] to be established
within the limits of the District
of Columbia, under the auspices
of the General Government, if that
Government should incline to ex-
-tend a fostering hand towards it,
—and until such seminary is estab-
-lished, and the funds arising on these
shares shall be required for its support,
my further will and desire is
that the profit accruing therefrom
shall whenever the dividends are
made, be laid out in purchasing
stock in the Bank of Columbia or
some other Bank at the discretion
of my Executors, or by the Treasurer
of the United States for the time being
under the direction of Congress, provided
that Honorable body should

patronize the measure. And the divi-
-dends proceeding from the purchase
of such Stock is to be vested in more
Stock and so on until a sum ade-
-quate to the accomplishment of the
object is obtained, of which I have
not the smallest doubt before many
years passes away, even if no aid
or *encouraged* is given by Legisla-
-tive authority or from any other source.

ITEM—The hundred shares which I held
in the James River Company I have
given and now confirm in perpetuity
to and for the use and benefit of Lib-
-erty Hall Academy[14] in the County of
Rockbridge, in the Commonwealth of *Virga*

ITEM—I release exonorate and discharge
the estate of my deceased brother, Samuel Washington from the payment,
of the money which is due to me for
the land I sold to Philip Pendleton
(lying in the County of Berkley) who
assigned the same to him the said
Samuel, who by agreement was to pay
me therefor.—And whereas by some
contract (the purport of which was
never communicated to me) between
the said Samuel and his son Thornton
Washington, the latter became pos-
-sessed of the aforesaid land without

any conveyance having passed from
me either to the said Pendleton the
said Samuel or the said Thornton and
without any consideration having
been made, by which neglect neither
the legal or equitable title has been
alienated;—it rests therefore with me
to declare my intentions concerning
the premises—And these are to
give and bequeath the said land to
whomsoever the said Thornton Washington
(who is also dead) devised the same
or to his heirs forever, if he
died intestate.—Exonerating the estate
of the said Thornton, equally with that
of the said Samuel from payment of
the purchase-money, which with In-
-terest agreeably to the original con-
-tract with the said Pendleton would
amount to more than a thousand pounds[15]
————And whereas two other sons of
my said deceased brother Samuel,—
namely, George Steptoe Washington
and Laurence Augustine •Washington
were by the decease of those to whose
care they were committed, brought under
my protection, and in consequence
have occasioned advances on my
part for their education at college
and other schools for their board
claothing and other incidental
expenses to the amount of near

five thousand dollars over and above
the sums furnished by their estate, *wch*
sum may be inconvenient for them
or their father's Estate to refund.—
I do for these reasons acquit them
and the said Estate from the pay-
-ment thereof.—My intention being
that all accounts between them and
me and their father's Estate and me
shall stand balanced.—

ITEM—The balance due to me from the
Estate of Bartholomew Dandridge de-
-ceased, (my wife's brother) and which
amounted on the first day of October,
1795, to Four hundred and twenty five
pounds (as will appear by an account
rendered by his deceased son, John
Dandridge, who was the acting Executor
of his father's will) I release & acquit
from the payment thereof.————And
the *negros* (then thirty three in num-
-ber) formerly belonging to the said
Estate who were taken in Execution,—
sold—and purchased in, on my
account in the year   and ever
since have remained in the posses-
-sion and to the use of Mary, widow
of the said Bartholomew Dandridge
with their increase, it is my will and
desire, shall continue and be in her
possession, without paying hire or making

compensation for the same for
the time past or to come during
her natural life, at the expiration
of which, I direct that all of them who
are forty years old and upwards shall
receive their freedom, all under that age
and above sixteen shall serve seven
years and no longer, and all under
sixteen years shall serve until they
are twenty-five years of age and then
be free.[16]——And to avoid disputes
respecting the ages of any of these *negros*
they are to be taken to the Court of the
County in which they reside and the
judgment thereof in this relation
shall be final and a record thereof
made, which may be adduced as
evidence at any time thereafter if
disputes should arise concerning the same.
——And I further direct that the heirs
of the said Bartholomew Dandridge shall
equally share the benefits arising from
the services of the said *negros* ac-
-cording to the tenor of this devise upon the
decease of their mother.

ITEM——If Charles Carter who inter-
-married with my niece, Betty Lewis, is not
sufficiently secured in the title to the lots
he had of me in the town of Fredericks-
-burg, it is my will and desire that my
Executors shall make such conveyances

of them as the law requires to render it
perfect.———

ITEM—To my nephew, Wm. Augustine
    Washington and his heirs (if he should
    conceive them to be objects worth prosecuting)
    and to his heirs a lot in the town of Man-
    -chester (opposite to Richmond) No. 265—
    drawn on my sole account and also
    the tenth of one or two hundred acre lots
    and two or three half-acre lots in the
    city and *vicinity* of Richmond, drawn in part-
    -nership with nine others, all in the
    lottery of the deceased William Byrd
    are given.—as is also a lot which I
    purchased of John Hood conveyed by
    William Willie and Saml Gordon
    Trustees of the said John Hood, num-
    -bered 139 in the town of Edenburgh in the
    County of Prince George, State of Virginia.

ITEM—To my nephew, Bushrod Washington[17]
    I give and bequeath all the papers
    in my possession which relate to my
    civil and military administration of the
    affairs of this Country :—I leave to him
    also such of my private papers as are
    worth preserving ;—and at the decease
    of—wife and before, if she is not
    inclined to retain them, I give and bequeath
    my library of Books and pamphlets of
    every kind.

G. Washington

ITEM—Having sold lands which I pos·
-sessed in the State of Pennsylvania
and part of a tract held in equal
right, with George Clinton, late Gover-
-nor of New York, in the State of New-
·York ;—My share of land and interest
in the great Dismal Swamp and a
tract of land which I owned in the
County of Gloucester ;—withholding
the legal titles thereto until the con-
-sideration money should be paid—
And having moreover leased and
conditionally sold, (as will appear
by the tenor of the said leases) all my
lands upon the Great *Kanhawa*[18] and
the tract upon Difficult Run in
the County of Loudon,[19] it is my will
and direction that whensoever the
contracts are fully and respectively
complied with according to the spirit,
true intent, and meaning thereof
on the part of the purchasers, their
heirs, or assigns, that then and in
that case conveyances are to be
made agreeably to the terms of the
said contracts and the money
arising therefrom when paid   ·
to be vested in Bank Stock, the
dividends whereof, as of that also which ·
is already vested therein, is to inure
to my said wife during her life
but the Stock its'self is to remain &

be subject to the general distribution
hereafter directed.————————

ITEM—To the Earl of Buchan I recom-
-mit, "The Box made of the Oak that
"sheltered the Great Sir William Wal-
"-lace after the battle of Falkirk"—
presented to me by his Lordship in
terms too flattering for me to repeat,—
with a request " To pass it, on the event
" of my decease to the man in my
" Country who should appear to merit
" it best, upon the same conditions
" that have induced him to send it
" to me."—Whether easy or not to
select *the man* who might comport
with his Lordship's opinion in this
respect, is not for me to say, but con-
-ceiving that no disposition of this
valuable curiosity, can be more eli-
-gable than the re-commitment of it
to his own cabinet agreeably to the
original design of the Goldsmith's—
Company of Edinburgh, who presen-
-ted it to him, and at his request,
consented that it should be transfered to
me; I do give and bequeath the same to
his Lordship, and in case of his de-
-cease, to his heir with my grateful
thanks for the distinguished honor
of presenting it to me, and more es-
-pecially for the favorable sentiments

with which he accompanied it——

ITEM—To my brother Charles Washington
   I give and bequeath the Gold-headed cane
   left me by Doct'r Franklin in his will—
   ——I add nothing to it because of the
   ample provision I have made for his
   issue——"——To the acquaintances and
   friends of my juvenile years, Lawrence
   Washington and Robert Washington[20] of
   Chotanck, I give my other two gold-headed
   canes, having my arms engraved on them,
   and to each (as they will be useful where
   they live), I leave one of the spy glasses
   which constituted part of my equipage
   during the late war——To my com-
   -patriot in arms and old and intimate
   friend Doct'r Craik,[21] I give my Bureau
   (or as the Cabinet makers called it Tam-
   -bour Secretary) and the circular chair,
   an appendage of my study——To
   Doct'r David Stuart I give my large
   shaving and dressing Table, and my Tel-
   -escope——To the Reverend now
   Bryan Lord Fairfax[22] I give a Bible in
   three large folio volumes with notes,
   presented to me by the Right Reverend
   Thomas Wilson, Bishop of Sodor & Man
   ——To General de la Fayette[23] I give
   a pair of finely wrought steel pistols
   taken from the enemy in the Revolutionary
   war——To my sisters in law

Hannah Washington, and Mildred Wash-
-ington ;—To my friends Eleanor Stuart,
Hannah Washington of Fairfield and
Elizabeth Washington of Hayfield I
give each a mourning Ring of the
value of one hundred dollars————These
bequests are not made for the intrins-
-ic value of them, but as *mementos*
of my esteem and regard————To Tobias
Lear[21] I give the use of the farm which
he now holds in virtue of a lease from
me to him and his deceased wife (for
and during their natural lives) free
from Rent during his life, at the ex-
-piration of which it is to be disposed
as is hereafter directed————To
Sally B Haynie (a distant relation
of mine) I give and bequeath three
hundred dollars————To Sarah
Green daughter of the deceased Thomas
Bishop and to Ann Walker, daughter
of Jno Alton, also deceased I give each
one hundred dollars, in consideration
of the attachment of their father
to me, each of whom having lived
nearly forty years in my family.—
————To each of my nephews William
Augustine Washington, George
Lewis, George Steptoe Washington.—
Bushrod Washington, and Samuel
Washington, I give one of the swords
or *cutteaux* of which I may die pos-

-sessed, and they are to *chuse* in the order
they are named.——These swords
are accompanied with an injunction
not to unsheath them for the pur-
-pose of shedding blood except it be
for self defence, or in defence of their
Country and it's rights, and in the latter
case to keep them unsheathed,
and prefer falling with them in their
hands to the relinquishment thereof.

AND NOW,
Having gone through these specific
devises, with explanations
for the more correct understanding
of the meaning and design of
them, I proceed to the distribution
of the more important parts of my
Estate, in manner following

First—To my nephew Bushrod Washington
and his heirs (partly in consider-
-ation of an intimation to his deceased
father, while we were bachelors and
he had kindly undertaken to super-
-intend my Estate, during my military
services in the former war between
Great Britian and France, that if I
should fall therein, Mt. Vernon
(then less extensive in domain than
at present) should become his prop-
-erty) I give and bequeath all that
part thereof which is comprehen-

-ded within the following limits—viz :—
Beginning at the ford of Dogue Run
near my mill and extending along the
road and bounded thereby as it now
goes, and ever has gone since my
recollection of it, to the ford of little hunting
Creek, at the gum spring until it comes
to a knowl opposite to an old road
which formerly passed through the
lower field of Muddy-Hole Farm;
at which, on the north side of the
said road are three red or Spanish oaks
marked as a corner, and a stone placed—
—thence by a line of trees to be marked
rectangular to the back line, or
outer boundary of the tract between
Thomas Mason and myself,—thence
with that line easterly, (*now double*
ditching with a post and rail fence
thereon) to the run of little hunting
Creek, thence with that run, which
is the boundary of the lands of
the late Humphrey Peake and *me*,
to the tide water of the said Creek
thence by that water to Potomac
River, thence with the River to the
mouth of Dogue Creek, and thence
with the said Dogue Creek to the
place of beginning, at the aforesaid ford,
containing upwards of Four thousand
acres, be the same more or less
together with the Mansion House,

and all other buildings and *improvemt*
thereon.————

ndly—In consideration of the consanguinity
between them and my wife, being as
as nearly related to her as to my self, as on
account of the affection I had for, and
the obligation I was under to their father
when living, who from his youth had attached
himself to my person and followed my
fortunes through the viscisitudes of the late
Revolution, afterwards devoting
his time to the superintendence of my
private concerns for many years whilst
my public employments rendered it im-
-practicable for me to do it myself
thereby affording me essential services, and
always performing them in a manner the
most filial and respectful; for
these reasons I say, I give and bequeath
to George Fayette Washington and Laurence
Augustine Washington[25] & their heirs my
Estate east of little hunting creek lying
on the River Potomac, including the
farm of 360, acres, leased to Tobias Lear
as noticed before and containing in
the whole, by deeds, Two thousand &
twenty seven acres be it more or less
which said Estate, it is my will and desire
should be equitably and advantageously
divided between them, according to
quantity, quality & other circumstances when

the youngest shall have arrived at the
age of twenty one years, by three judicious
and disinterested men, one to be
chosen by each of the brothers and the
third by these two,—In the mean time
if the termination of my wifes interest
therein should have ceased the profits,
arising therefrom are to be applied
for their joint uses and benefit

Third—And whereas it has always been
my intention, since my expectation of
having issue has ceased, to consider
the grand children of my wife in the
same light as I do my own relations
and to act a friendly part by them,
more especially by the two whom we have
reared from their earliest infancy,
namely, Eleanor Parke Custis
and George Washington Parke Custis;[26]
and whereas the former of these
hath lately intermarried with Lawrence
Lewis, a son of my deceased sister
Betty Lewis, by which union the
inducement to provide for them both
has been increased.—Wherefore
I give and bequeath to the said Lawrence
Lewis and Eleanor Parke Lewis, his wife,
and their heirs, the residue of my
Mount Vernon Estate, not already
devised to my nephew Bushrod Washing-
-ton comprehended within the fol-

-lowing description.—viz—all the land
north of the Road leading from the ford
of Dogue Run to the Gum Spring as de-
-scribed in the devise of the other part of the
tract to Bushrod Washington until
it comes to the stone and three red or
Spanish oaks on the knowl.—thence
with the rectangular line to the back
line (between Mr Mason and *me*)—thence
with that line westerly, along the new
double ditch to Dogue Run, by the tumbling
dam of my mill,———thence with the
said Run to the ford aforementioned;
—to which I add all the land I possess
west of the said Dogue Run & Dogue Crk
bounded, Easterly & Southerly thereby—together
with the Mill, Distillery and all
other houses and improvements on the
premises making together about
two thousand acres be it more or less

Fourth—Actuated by the principle already
mentioned, I give and bequeath
to George Washington Parke Custis the
Grand son of my wife and my ward
and to his heirs, the tract I hold on
four mile Run in the *vicinity* of
Alexandria containing one thousd
two hundred acres more or less;[27]—&
my entire Square, number twenty
one, in the City of Washington.—

Fifth——All the rest and residue of my
    Estate, real and personal, not disposed
    of in manner aforesaid—In whatso-
    -ever consisting—wheresoever lying, and
    whensoever found—a Schedule of which
    as far as is recollected, with a reason-
    -able estimate of its value is hereunto
    annexed—I desire may be sold by my
    Executors at such times—in such man-
    -ner, and on such credits (if an equal
    valid and satisfactory distribution of the
    specific property cannot be made
    without) as, in their judgment
    shall be most conducive to the inter-
    -est of the parties concerned, and the
    monies arising therefrom to be divided
    into twenty three equal parts
    and applied as follows—viz :—

        To William Augustine Washingtor
    Elizabeth Spotswood, Jane Thornton,
    and the heirs of Ann Ashton; son and
    daughters of my deceased brother
    Augustine Washington, I give and
    bequeath four parts—that is—one part
    to each of them.——"——"——"——

        To Fielding Lewis, George Lewis
    Robert Lewis, Howell Lewis & Betty
    Carter, sons and daughter of my de-
    -ceased sister Betty Lewis I give & be-
    -queath five other parts—one to each of them

        To George Steptoe Washington
    Laurence Augustine Washington, *Harriot*

G Washington

Parks, and the heirs of Thornton Wash-
-ington, sons and daughter of my deceased
brother Samuel Washington, I give
and bequeath other four parts, one
part to each of them.————

  To Corbin Washington, and the
heirs of Jane Washington, son & daugh-
-ter of my deceased brother John Augus-
-tine Washington, I give and bequeath two
parts ;—one part to each of them;————

  To Samuel Washington, Francis
Ball & Mildred Hammond, son and daugh-
-ters of my brother Charles Washington
I give and bequeath three parts—one part
to each of them.————And to George Fayette
Washington, Charles Augustine Washington
and Maria Washington, sons and
daughter of my deceased nephew, Geo :
Augustine Washington, I give one other
part—that is—to each a third of that part

  To Elizabeth Parke Law, Martha
Parke Peter, and Eleanor Parke Lewis
I give and bequeath three other parts—
that is, a part to each of them.————

  And to my nephews Bushrod
Washington & Lawrence Lewis,—and to
my ward, the grand son of my wife,
I give and bequeath one other part ;—that
is a third thereof to each of them—And
if it should so happen, that any of the
persons whose names are here ennu-
-merated (unknown to me) should now

be deceased, or should die before me,
that in either of these cases, the heirs
of such deceased, person shall, not-
-withstanding derive all the benefit of
the bequest, in the same manner as if
he, or she, was actually living at the time
          And by way of advice, I recom-
-mend it to my Executors not to be pre-
-cipitate in disposing of the landed
property (herein directed to be sold)
if from temporary causes the sale
thereof should be dull, experience
having fully evinced, that the price of
land (especially above the Falls of the
Rivers & on the Western Waters) have
been progressively rising, and cannot
be long checked in it's increasing
value.——and I particularly rec-
-commend it to such of the Legatees (under
this clause of my will) as can make
it convenient, to take each a share of my
stock in the Potomac Company in
preference to the amount of what
it might sell for; being thoroughly
convinced myself, that no uses to which
the money can be applied will
be so productive as the Tolls arising
from this navigation when in full
operation (and this from the nature
of things it must be 'ere long) and
more especially if that of the Shanan-
-doah is added thereto.—

The family Vault at Mount Ver-
-non requiring repairs, and being
improperly situated besides, I desire
that a new one of Brick, and upon
a larger scale, may be built at the
foot of what is commonly called the
Vineyard Inclosure,—on the ground
which is marked out.[28]—In which my
remains, with those of my deceased
relatives (now in the Old Vault) and
such others of my family as may
chuse to be entombed there, may be
deposited.—And it is my express
desire that my Corpse may be inter-
-red in a private manner, without
parade or funeral oration.——

Lastly—I constitute and appoint my
dearly beloved wife Martha Wash-
-ington, my nephews William Augus-
-tine Washington, Bushrod Washington
George Steptoe Washington, Samuel
Washington & Lawrence Lewis, &
my ward, George Washington Parke
Custis (when he shall have arrived
at the age of twenty years) Executrix &
Executors of this Will & Testament,—
—In the construction of which it will
readily be perceived that no professional
character has been consulted
or has had any agency in the draught
—and that, although it has occupied

many of my leisure hours to digest
& to *through* it into its present form, it
may notwithstanding, appear crude
and incorrect—But having endeavored
to be plain and explicit in
all the Devises—even at the expense
of prolixity, perhaps of tautology,
I hope, and trust, that no disputes
will arise concerning them ; but
if contrary to expectation the case should
be otherwise from the want of legal ex-
-pression, or the usual technical terms
or because too much or too little ; has been
said on any of the devises
to be consonant with law, my will
and direction expressly is, that all
disputes (if unhappily any should
arise) shall be decided by three
impartial and intelligent men, known
for their probity and good understand-
-ing; two to be chosen by the
disputants, each having the choice
of one, and the third by those two.—
which three men thus chosen, shall
unfettered by Law, or legal construc-
-tions, declare their sense of the
Testator's intention ; and such
decision is, to all intents and purposes
to be as binding on the Parties
as if it had been given in
the Supreme Court of the United
States.[29]—

In witness of all and of
each of the things herein contained
I have set my hand
and seal this ninth
day of July, in the year
one thousand seven hun-
-dred and ninety* and of the
Independence of the
United States, the Twenty
fourth.

GWashington

* It appears the Testator omitted the word "nine."

279577

SCHEDULE OF PROPERTY *comprehended in the foregoing Will, which is directed to be sold, and some of it, conditionally is sold; with descriptive and explanitory notes relative thereto.*———

IN VIRGINIA.

	ACRES.	PRICE.	DOLLARS.
LOUDOUN COUNTY—			
Difficult Run......................	300		6.666 (*a*)
LOUDOUN & FAUQUIER—			
Ashby's Bent.....................	2,481	$10	24.810 } (*b*)
Chattin's Run	885	8	7.080 }
BERKLEY—			
So. Fork of Bullskin...........	1,600 }		
Head of Evan's M...........	453 }		
In Wormley's Line...........	183 }		
	2,236	20	44.720 (*c*)
FREDERICK—			
Bought from Mercer...........	571	20	11.420 (*d*)
HAMPSHIRE—			
On Potk. River above B.....	240	15	3.600 (*e*)
GLOUCESTER—			
On North River..	400	*abt*	3.600 (*f*)
NANSEMOND—			
Near Suffolk ⅓ of } 1119 Acres........ }	373	8	2.984 (*g*)
GREAT DISMAL SWAMP—			
My dividend thereof		abt	20.000 (*h*)
OHIO RIVER—			
Round Bottom.........	587		
Little *Kanhawa*................	2,314		
	2,901		$124.880

SCHEDULE—*Continued.*

	ACRES.	PRICE.	DOLLARS.	
Amount brought over.	2,901		124.880	
16 miles lower down............	2,448			
Opposite Big Bent...............	4,395			
	9,744	10	97,440	(*i*)
GREAT *Kanhawa*—				
Near the mouth west..........	10,990			
East Side above.................	7,276			
Mouth of Cole River..........	2,000			
Opposite thereto...............	2,950			
Burning Spring.................	125			
	23,341		200.000	(*k*)
MARYLAND—				
Charles County.................	600	6	3,600	(*l*)
Montgomery County..........	519	12	6.228	(*m*)
PENNSYLVANIA—				
Great Meadows.................	234	6	1.404	(*n*)
NEW YORK—				
Mohawk River *abt*.............	1,000	6	6.000	(*o*)
NORTH WEST TERRITORY—				
On little Miami.................	839			
Ditto	977			
Ditto	1,235			
	3,051	5	15.251	(*p*)
KENTUCKY—				
Rough Creek...................	3,000			
Ditto adjoin'g..............	2,000			
	5,000	2	10.000	(*q*)

Lots—viz :—

CITY OF WASHINGTON—

Two near the *Capital Sqr*........... 634 }

Cost $963, and with *Buildgs*.......   15.000 (*r*)

Carried over 479.803

SCHEDULE OF PROPERTY *comprehended in the foregoing Will, which is directed to be sold, and some of it, conditionally is sold; with descriptive and explanitory notes relative thereto.*————

IN VIRGINIA.

	ACRES.	PRICE.	DOLLARS.	
LOUDOUN COUNTY—				
Difficult Run.....................	300		6.666	(*a*)
LOUDOUN & FAUQUIER—				
Ashby's Bent.....................	2,481	$10	24.810 ⎫	(*b*)
Chattin's Run	885	8	7.080 ⎭	
BERKLEY—				
So. Fork of Bullskin...........	1,600 ⎫			
Head of Evan's M.............	453 ⎬			
In Wormley's Line...........	183 ⎭			
	2,236	20	44.720	(*c*)
FREDERICK—				
Bought from Mercer...........	571	20	11.420	(*d*)
HAMPSHIRE—				
On Potk. River above B.....	240	15	3.600	(*e*)
GLOUCESTER—				
On North River.	400	*abt*	3.600	(*f*)
NANSEMOND—				
Near Suffolk ⅓ of ⎫ 1119 Acres........ ⎭	373	8	2.984	(*g*)
GREAT DISMAL SWAMP—				
My dividend thereof		abt	20.000	(*h*)
OHIO RIVER—				
Round Bottom...................	587			
Little *Kanhawa*...............	2,314			
	2,901		$124.880	

SCHEDULE—*Continued.*

	ACRES.	PRICE.	DOLLARS.
Amount brought over.	2,901		124.880
16 miles lower down...........	2,448		
Opposite Big Bent..............	4,395		
	9,744	10	97,440 *(i)*

GREAT *Kanhawa—*

	ACRES.	PRICE.	DOLLARS.
Near the mouth west.........	10,990		
East Side above................	7,276		
Mouth of Cole River..........	2,000		
Opposite thereto	2,950		
Burning Spring.................	125		
	23,341		200.000 *(k)*

MARYLAND—

	ACRES.	PRICE.	DOLLARS.
Charles County.................	600	6	3,600 *(l)*
Montgomery County...........	519	12	6.228 *(m)*

PENNSYLVANIA—

	ACRES.	PRICE.	DOLLARS.
Great Meadows.................	234	6	1.404 *(n)*

NEW YORK—

	ACRES.	PRICE.	DOLLARS.
Mohawk River *abt*.............	1,000	6	6.000 *(o)*

NORTH WEST TERRITORY—

	ACRES.	PRICE.	DOLLARS.
On little Miami.................	839		
Ditto	977		
Ditto	1,235		
	3,051	5	15.251 *(p)*

KENTUCKY—

	ACRES.	PRICE.	DOLLARS.
Rough Creek	3,000		
Ditto adjoin'g.........	2,000		
	5,000	2	10.000 *(q)*

Lots—viz:—

CITY OF WASHINGTON—

	ACRES.	PRICE.	DOLLARS.
Two near the *Capital Sqr*........... 634 ⎫			
Cost $963, and with *Buildgs*....... ⎭			15.000 *(r)*

Carried over 479.803

SCHEDULE—*Continued.*

DOLLARS.

Amt. brought over................ 479.803

LOTS—CITY OF WASHINGTON—

No. 5, 12, 13 & 14, the 3 last water ⎫
lots on the Eastern Branch ⎪
in Sqr 667, containing together ⎬ 4.132 (*s*)
34,438 Sqr feet at 12 cts ⎭

ALEXANDRIA—

Corner of Pitt and Prince Strts ⎫
half an acre—laid out into ⎪
buildgs 3 or 4 of *wch* are let ⎬ 4.000 (*t*)
on *grd* Rent at $3 pr foot ⎭

WINCHESTER—

A lot in the Town, of half an ⎫
acre & another on the Commons of ⎬ 400 (*u*)
about 6 acres—supposed ⎭

BATH—OR WARM SPRINGS—

. Two well situated & had buil- ⎫
-dings to the amount of £150. ⎭ 800 (u)

STOCK.

UNITED STATES 6 PR CTS........ 3,746
Do   defered 1,873 ⎫ 2,500
        3 prcts 2,946 ⎭
                                       ⎯⎯⎯
                                       6.246 (*x*)

POTOMAC COMPANY—

24 Shares cost ea £100 *Sterl'g*......... 10.666 (*y*)

JAMES RIVER COMPANY—

5 Shares each cost $100............... 500 (*z*)

BANK OF COLUMBIA—

170 Shares—$40 each.................... 6.800 ⎫
BANK OF ALEXANDRIA—besides ⎫   ⎬ (*&*)
20 to the Free School 5 ⎭   1.000 ⎭

                                       ⎯⎯⎯
                                       514.347

SCHEDULE—*Continued.*

Amt. brought over.. ....   514.347

STOCK—living—viz.—

1 Covering horse, 5 *Colt*
horses—4 Riding do—six
brood mares—20 work-
-ing horses & mares,—2
Covering Jacks & 3 young ones
10 she asses—42 working
mules—15 younger ones
329 head of horned cattle   15,653
640 head of Sheep, and
a large stock of hogs, the
precise number unknown—
☞ My manager has estima-
-ted this live stock at £7,000
but I shall set it down in
order to make *sd* sum at—

Aggregate amt: $530.000

NOTES.

(*a*)   ⸸ This tract for the size of it is valu-
-able ; more for it's situation than the qual-
-ity of it's soil, though that is good for Farm-
-ing, with a considerable portion of gr'd
that might, very easily, be improved into
meadow.—It *lyes* on the great Road from
the City of Washington, Alexandria and
George Town to *Leesburgh* & Winchester,
at Difficult bridge—nineteen miles from
Alexandria—less from the City & George-
Town, and not more than three from Ma-
-tildaville at the Great Falls of Potomac—

There is a valuable seat on the Prem-
-ises—and the whole is conditionally—
sold for the sum annexed in the Schedule

(*b*)   What the selling prices of lands in
the *vicinity* of these two tracts are I
know not ; but compared with those
above the ridge, and others below them
the value annexed will appear mode-
-rate——a less one would not obtain them
from me.——

(*c*)   The surrounding land, not supe-
-rior in soil, situation or properties of
any sort, sell currently at from twenty to
thirty dollars an acre.——The lowest—
price is affixed to these

(*d*)   The observations made in the last
note applies equally to this *tract tract*

being in the *vicinity* of them, and of sim-
-ilar quality, *altho* it *lye's* in another County

(e)   This tract though small, is extremely
valuable——it *lyes* on the Potomac River,
about twelve miles above the Town of Bath (or
Warm Springs) and is in the shape of a
horse-shoe, the River running almost
around it.—Two hundred acres of it *is*
rich low grounds; with a great abun-
-dance of the largest and finest Walnut
Trees, which with the produce of the soil
might (by means of the improved navi-
-gation of the Potomac) be brought to a
shipping port with more ease and at *a*
smaller expense than that which is
transported 30 miles, only by land

(*f*) This tract is of second rate
Gloucester low ground—it has no
improvement thereon, but *lyes* on navigable
water abounding in fish and oysters:
it was received in payment of a debt
(carrying interest) and valued in the
year 1789, by an impartial gentleman
to £800.—N. B.   It has *lettely* been sold
and there is due thereon, a balance
equal to what is annexed—the Schedule

(*g*)   These 373 acres *are* the third part
of undivided purchases made by the
deceased Fielding Lewis, Thomas Walker
and myself, on full conviction that

they would become valuable.——the land
lye's on the road from Suffolk to Norfolk
touches (if I am not mistaken) some part
of the navigable water of Nansemond River—
borders on—and comprehends part of
the rich Dismal Swamp; is capable of
great improvement;——and from it's situ-
-ation must become extremely valuable.

(*h*)   This is an undivided interest *wch*
I held in the Great Dismal Swamp Company,
containing about 400 acres, with my
part of the Plantation and Stock thereon
belonging to the Company in the *s'd* Swamp

(*i*)   These several Tracts of land are
of the first quality on the Ohio River in
the parts where they are situated;—being
almost, if not altogether, River bottoms.—

——The smallest of these Tracts is ac-
-tually sold at ten dollars an acre, but the
consideration therefor, not received,
the rest are equally valuable, and will
sell as high, especially that which *lye's* just
below the little *Kanhawa*, and is oppo-
-site to a thick settlement on the west side the River

——The four tracts have an aggregate
breadth upon the River of Sixteen miles
and is bounded thereby that distance

(*k*)   These tracts are situated on the
Great *Kanhawa* River, and the first

NOTES.

four are bounded thereby for more
than forty miles.—It is acknowledged
by all who have seen them (and of the
tract containing 10,990 acres which I
have been on myself, I can assert) that
there is no richer, or more valuable
land in all that Region ;—They are
conditionally sold for the sum mentioned
in the schedule—that is $200.000
and if the terms of that sale are not
complied with, they will command con-
-siderably more.——The tract of which
the 125 acres is a moiety, was taken
up by General Andrew Lewis and myself
for and on account of a bituminous Spring
which it contains, of so inflamable a na-
-ture as to burn as freely as spirits, and
is as nearly difficult to extinguish.

(*l*)　　　I am but little acquainted with
this land, although I have once been on
it.—It was received (many years since)
in discharge of a debt due to me from
Daniel Janifer Adams, at the value
annexed thereto, and must be worth
more.——It is very level, *lyes* near
the River Potomac

(*m*)　　　This tract *lyes* about 30 miles
above the City of Washington not far
from *Kittoctan*.—It is good farming
land, and by those who are well ac-

-quainted with it, I am informed that it
would sell at twelve or $15. pr acre

(*n*)   This land is valuable on account
of it's local situation and other properties.—
—It affords an exceeding good stand
on Braddock's Road from Fort Cumberland
to *Pittsburgh* and besides a fertile soil
possesses a large quantity of natural
meadow fit for the scythe.—It is distin-
-guished by the appellation of the Great Mea-
-dows, where the first action with the French
in the year 1754 was fought

(*o*)   This is the moiety of about 2000 *acrs*
which remains unsold of 6071 acres
on the Mohawk River, (Montgomery Ct'y)
in a Patent granted to Daniel Coxe in
the Township of *Coxebourgh & Carolaca*
as will appear by deed from Marinus
Willet & wife to George Clinton (late
Governor of New York) and myself; The lat-
-ter sales have been at six dollars an acre
and what remains unsold will *fetch* that,
or more

(*p*)   The quality of these lands & their
situation may be known by the surveyor's
certificates, which are filed along with
the patents—They *lye* in the *vicinity* of
Cincinnati, one tract near the mouth of
the little Miami, another seven, & the third

NOTES.

ten miles up the same—I have been
informed that they will readily command
more than they are estimated at.————

(*q*)   For the description of these tracts
in detail, see General Spottswood's letters
filed with the other papers relating to them————
————Besides the general good qual-
-ity of the land, there is a valuable
bank of Iron Ore theron ;—which when
the settlement becomes more populous
(and settlers are moving that way
very fast) will be found very valuable,
as the rough creek, a branch of
Green River affords ample water for
furnaces and forges.

LOTS,—Viz :

CITY OF WASHINGTON—

(*r*)   The two lots near the *Capital* in
Square 634, cost me $963 only, but in
this price I was favoured on condition
that I should build two brick houses,
three storys high each ;—without
this reduction, the selling price of those
lots would have cost me about $1350.
————These lots with the buildings
thereon when completed will stand me in
$15.000 at least

(*s*)   Lots No. 5, 12, 13 & 14 on the Eastern
Branch are advantageously situated
on the water, and although many lots

much less convenient, have sold a great
deal higher, I will rate these at 12 cts
the Square foot only.

ALEXANDRIA.

(*t*)　　　For this lot, though unimproved
I have refused $3500. it has since been
laid off into proper sized lots for building
on, three or four of which are let on
ground Rent forever at three dollars
a foot on the street, and this price
is asked for both fronts on Pitt & Prin-
-cess streets.——

WINCHESTER.

(*u*)　　　As neither the lot in the Town
or common have any improvements
on them it is not easy to fix a price,
but as both are well situated it is
presumed the price annexed to them
in the Schedule is a reasonable *valu*

BATH.

(*v*)　　　The lots in Bath (two adjoining) cost
me to the best of my recollection, between
fifty and sixty pounds, 20 years ago & the
buildings thereon, £150 more.—whether
property there has increased or decreased
in it's value, and in what condition
the houses are, I am ignorant,
but suppose they are not valued too high

STOCKS.

(*x*)   These are the sums which are
actually funded, and though no more
in the aggregate than $7566. stand me
in at least Ten thousand pounds in Vir-
-ginia money, being the amount of
bonded and other debts due to me, and
discharged during the war, when
money had depreciated in that ratio
and was so settled by public authority.

(*y*)   The value annexed to these shares
is what they have actually cost me,
. and is the price affixed by law:—and
although the present selling price is
under par, my advice to the Legatees
(for whose benefit they are intended,
especially those who can afford to *lye*
out of the money) is that each should
take and hold one ; there being a
moral certainty of a great and in-
-creasing profit arising from them
in the course of a few years——

(*z*)   It is supposed that the shares
in the James River Company must also
be productive—But of this I
can give no decided opinion
for want of more accurate information.

(&)   These are nominal prices
of the Shares of the Banks of Alex-

-andria & Columbia, the selling prices
vary according to circumstances
but as the stock usually divided from
eight to ten per cent per annum, they
must be worth the former, at least,
so long as the Banks are conceived
to be secure, although circumstan-
-ces may sometimes below it

The value of the live stock
depends more upon the quality than
quantity of the different species of it
and this again upon the demand,
and judgment or fancy of purchasers.

Mount Vernon,

9 *July,* 1799.

At a Court held for the County of Fairfax
the 20th day of January 1800, this last Will and
Testament of George Washington, deceased, late
President of the United States of America, was pre-
-sented in Court by George Steptoe Washington, Samuel
Washington, & Lawrence Lewis, three of the
Executors therein named, who made oath thereto,
and the same being proved by the oaths of Charles
Little, Charles Simms and Ludwell Lee, to be in
the true hand writing of the said Testator, as also
the *Scædule* thereto annexed, and the said Will,
being sealed and signed by him is on motion, Ordered
to be Recorded——And the said Executors
having given Security and performed what the Laws
require, a Certificate is granted them for obtaining
a probate thereof in due form.

TESTE:

G. DENEALE, *Cl: Fx:*

R. L. H. *fo:* 1

    Ex^d * by

G. DENEALE, *Cl: Fx:*

---

* This endorsement of the clerk is intended to
represent that the will &c is " Recorded Liber
H, folio 1 and Examined.♥

NOTES OF THE PUBLISHER.

Note 1, Page 1.—GEORGE WASHINGTON. The progenitor of the Washingtons, of whom this Testator was one, seems to have been William De Hertbern, of Norman origin, whom we find in the century succeeding the conquest of William, in possession of certain estates held of the Bishop de Pusaz in knight's fee, situated in Durham, England. The surname De Hertbern was taken from a village on the Palatinate which he held of the bishop, supposed to be the same now called Hartburn on the banks of the Tees. The first actual mention we find of the family is in the Bolden Book.* In this it is stated that William de Hertbern had exchanged his village of Hertburn for the manor and village of Wessyngton in the same diocese, paying the bishop certain quit-rents, &c.— This occurred in 1183, the earliest data to which we can trace, and it seems that from this period forward the family assumed the name of De Wessyngton.† About the time of the reign of Henry VI. the *de* or *d'* was generally dropped from surnames, and the title of *armiger, esquire,* amongst the heads of families, and *generosus,* or *gentleman,* among younger sons substituted; and we find the family name of the Testator to vary from Wassyngton to Wassington, Washington, and finally to Washington. The branch of the family to which our Washington immediately belongs sprang from Lawrence Washington, Esq., of Gray's Inn, son of John Washington, of Warton in Lancashire. This Laurence Washington received from Henry VIII., in 1538, the grant of the manor of Sulgrave, in Northamptonshire, and was known in 1620 as "Washington's Manor." We have little note of the Sulgrave branch of the family after the death of Charles I. and the exile of his successor. In 1655 the persecutions of Cromwell drove many of the adherents of the house of Stuart from England, and many of their party who had no share in the conspiracy, sought refuge in other lands. This may have been the case with two brothers, John and Andrew Washington, great grandsons of the grantee of Sulgrave. These brothers arrived in Virginia in 1657, and purchased lands in Westmoreland county, on the northern neck, between the Potomac and Rappahannock rivers. John married a Miss Anne Pope, of the same county, and resided at Bridges Creek,‡ near where it falls into the Potomac. We afterwards find him as Colonel of Virginia forces, co-operating with those of Maryland against a band of Seneca Indians. His grandson, Augustine Washington, the father of our Washington, was born at Bridge's Creek in 1694. He was twice married: first (April 20, 1715,) to Jane, daughter of Caleb Butler, Esq., of Westmoreland county, by whom he had four children, of whom only two, Laurence and Augustine, survived the years of childhood; their mother died November 24, 1728, and was interred near the remains of Col. Washington, at Bridge's Creek. On the 6th of March, 1730, he married in second nuptials Mary, daughter of Colonel Ball, the belle of the Northern Neck. By her he had four sons, George, Samuel, John Augustine, and Charles; and two daughters, Elizabeth, or Betty as she was commonly called, and Mildred, who died in infancy.

George, the eldest, the American soldier, statesman and patriot, was born 22d February, (11th, O. S.,) in the old Washington homestead on Bridge's Creek.

---

* Irving's Life of Washington, Vol. I, folio 4.

† Probably of Saxon origin. We find the village of Wassengtone mentioned in a Saxon charter granted by Edgar, 973, to Thorney Abbey, prior to the conquest.—*Irving*, I. 5.

‡ Bridges Creek, for generations, was the family place of sepulture.

This house commanded a beautiful view over many miles of the Potomac, and opposite shore of Maryland; it contained four rooms on the ground floor, and others in the attic. Such was the birth place of our great and loved Washington. Not a vestige now remains of it; only a stone * marks the site of the "old low-pitched farm house," and an inscription denotes its being the birth place of Washington.

In giving the genealogy of the Washington family, we have been as brief as possible; though embracing a period of six generations and upwards, we deem it needless to claim the attention of the reader further, as we could only borrow from the volumes already written by such authors as Spark, Marshall, and Irving.

Note 2, Page 1.—"MT. VERNON." Familiar as this American Mecca is to all, it is useless to add either engraving or description here. It is sufficient to say that this spot, the chosen home of Washington, and the place of his death and burial, is in the county of Fairfax, Virginia, lying on the Potomac river, 8 miles below Alexandria, and sixteen from Washington City. It was inherited by Laurence Washington from Augustine Washington, his father and the father of George Washington, in April, 1743, and was named by him, Mount Vernon, in honor of Admiral Vernon, of the English Navy, with whom he had been intimate in the campaigns in West Indies in 1741–42. After his death (26th July, 1752,) Mount Vernon descended to George Washington. It was willed by General Washington to his nephew, Bushrod Washington, son of John Augustine Washington, after whose death it descended to his son, John Augustine Washington (who was, while aid to General R. E. Lee with the rank of Colonel, killed near Cheat Mountain, in September, 1861.)

In 1855, Mrs. Ann Pamelia Cunningham and other ladies conceived the plan of forming an association, the object of which should be the purchase of Mount Vernon, or that portion including the dwelling, tomb, and present steamboat landing. In the Spring of 1856 the matter was brought before the Legislature of Virginia, then in session, and on the 17th March, 1856, the association was incorporated as "The Mount Vernon Ladies' Association of the Union" and is as follows, viz.:

"CHAP. 298.—An ACT to incorporate the Mount Vernon ladies association of the Union, and to authorize the purchase of a part of Mount Vernon.

Passed March 17, 1856.

Whereas, it appears to the general assembly, that the ladies of the United States, acting in the name and style of the Mount Vernon ladies association of the Union, have undertaken to raise, by individual subscription, a fund to purchase and improve two hundred acres of Mount Vernon, with the generous and patriotic design that the estate so purchased shall include the late mansion as well as the tomb of General George Washington, and shall thereby be converted into public property, and forever held by the state of Virginia, sacred to the memory of the Father of his country: and whereas it also appears that there has been already a large sum subscribed and paid in by them for the purposes aforesaid, and that it is desired by said association that the State of Virginia shall receive said money, and hold and take care thereof for said association until an amount is obtained sufficient to accomplish said purchase:

1. Be it therefore by the general assembly enacted, that the treasurer of this commonwealth shall receive into the treasury all the money or moneys offered to him by the Mount Vernon ladies association of the Union, or by others in their behalf, and shall keep the same therein, except upon orders from the governor of Virginia. The fund so raised shall be styled and known by the name of the Mount Vernon ladies association fund. But nothing herein shall be construed so as to make it obligatory on said association, or any branch or agency thereof, in any state, to pay or deposit their money in said treasury.

---

* Placed there by George W. P. Custis.

2. The said treasurer shall keep separate accounts for this fund, and shall report its amount and condition to the governor every six months, and to the general assembly at every session held while said fund is in his custody. He shall also procure, at the cost of the commonwealth, two books of proper size, and shall transcribe into each, in fair hand, the names of the contributors to the fund, and the sum contributed by each, so far as those names and respective sums are furnished to him by said association. One of these books shall be kept forever in the archives of Virginia, and the other shall be deposited in the least destructible part of any monument or other improvement which may be hereafter erected on said Mount Vernon.

3. The governor of this commonwealth is hereby authorized and required to obtain, as soon as practicable, from John A. Washington, his heirs or assigns, a contract, signed and sealed by him, and binding him to convey, by proper deed to the state of Virginia, two hundred acres of land, out of said Mount Vernon, at any time within five years from the passage of this act, that the said governor pays to him the sum of two hundred thousand dollars.

4. The said deed of conveyance shall be in fee simple, reserving to the said grantor to inter, in or around the family vault, any and all members of the Washington family, legally descended from the said John A. Washington ; and the further right to maintain perpetually the interment of those already there. It shall recite that the purchase money was paid by the ladies of the United States, acting in the name and style of the Mount Vernon ladies association of the Union, and at their instance the said conveyance is made to the state of Virginia. And it shall covenant that the estate so conveyed shall be kept free from injury and desecration, and held in trust for said association, forever sacred to the memory of George Washington, whose mortal remains shall be kept perpetually thereon. And then upon this further trust, that the said estate shall be subject to visitation by the state of Virginia and to such proper and becoming improvements as the said association shall desire and determine and make. But in default of said association making such proper and becoming improvements or keeping the same in proper repair, upon such default being found by a board of visitors, then said estate shall be subject to improvement and repair at the pleasure of the state of Virginia ; and to this end, the possession of said estate shall vest in said state.

5. The said two hundred acres of ground shall include the tomb of George Washington, mansion, garden, grounds, and the wharf and landing now constructed on the Potomac river.

6. The governor shall invest the money paid into the treasury on account of said association, as soon as convenient after he has notice thereof, in stock, or in loans to individuals or to corporate bodies, on good and sufficient security, real and personal; at an interest of six per centum per annum, to be paid semi annually, as may to said governor seem best ; and the profits arising from such investment shall also be semiannually invested, or as soon thereafter as the same can be profitably done. And the said governor shall so continue to invest said fund and the profits thereof until the same amount to the sum of two hundred thousand dollars : and shall thereupon proceed to pay the same to said John A. Washington, and receive from him the aforesaid deed of conveyance. The governor shall in like manner invest all and any money of said association which is paid into said treasury for the purpose of improving said estate.

7. The said association may charge, receive and collect any fee which may be prescribed, not exceeding twenty-five cents from each and every person over ten years of age, who may land at and visit Mount Vernon and the grave, tomb or other place containing the remains of General Washington ; but no greater sum or fee shall be charged or collected in any case.

8. The governor of Virginia shall annually appoint and commission five fit and proper men, who shall constitute a board of visitors for Mount Vernon, with the ordinary powers of a board of visitors, whose duty it shall be to visit that place and examine and faithfully report to the governor all the proceedings of said association touching Mount Vernon, and the manner in which they comply or fail to comply with this act and other laws of the land. The expenses of

said board shall be paid out of the treasury of this commonwealth in the same manner that the expenses of other boards of visitors are paid.

9. The said association are hereby declared and made a body politic and corporate for the purpose of raising money to purchase and improve the aforesaid two hundred acres of land out of Mount Vernon, and to possess and manage the same as indicated and provided for in this act, under the name and style of The Mount Vernon Ladies Association of the Union; and shall be subject to all the provisions and entitled to all the rights, powers, privileges and immunities prescribed in the first and second sections of the fifty-sixth chapter of the Code of Virginia, in so far as the same are applicable to and not inconsistent with the provisions of this act. But the said association shall not be entitled to the benefit of the foregoing provisions in this section until they shall have prepared a constitution and by-laws for said corporation, and have the same approved by the governor of this state; and shall also file a copy thereof, so approved, in the office of the secretary of the commonwealth.

10. This act shall be in force from its passage."

And on the 19th day of March, 1858, was by said Legislature amended as follows, viz.:

1. Be it enacted by the general assembly, that the act entitled an act to incorporate the "Mount Vernon Ladies Association of the Union" and to authorize the purchase of a part of Mount Vernon, passed March 17, 1856, be amended and re-enacted so as to read as follows:

"§ 1. The Mount Vernon Ladies Association of the Union as heretofore organized, shall be and they are hereby constituted a body politic and corporate, under the name and style of The Ladies Mount Vernon Association of the Union; and by this name and style, shall be subject to all the provisions, and entitled to all the rights, powers and privileges and immunities prescribed by existing laws in so far as the same are applicable to like corporations, and not inconsistent with this act.

"§ 2. It shall be lawful for the said Mount Vernon Ladies Association of the Union, to purchase, hold and improve two hundred acres of Mount Vernon, including the late mansion as well as the tomb of George Washington, together with the garden, grounds and wharf and landing now constructed on the Potomac river; and to this end they may receive from the owner and proprietor of the said land a deed in fee simple: and shall have and exercise full power over the use and management of the same, as they may by by-laws and rules declare, provided however, that the said Mount Vernon Ladies Association of the Union, shall not have power to alien the said land, or any part thereof, or to lease the same without the consent of the general assembly of Virginia first had and obtained.

"§ 3. The capital stock of the said Mount Vernon Ladies Association of the Union shall not, including the two hundred acres of land aforesaid, exceed the sum of five hundred dollars. The said association, in contracting with the proprietor of the same, may covenant with him so as to reserve to him the right to inter the remains of such persons whose remains are in the vault at Mount Vernon as are not now interred, and to place the said vault in such a secure and permanent condition as he shall see fit, and to inclose the same so as not to include more than a half acre of land; and the said vault, the remains in and around it, and the inclosure, shall never be removed nor disturbed, nor shall any other person hereafter ever be interred or entombed within the said vault or enclosure.

"§ 4. The said property herein authorized to be purchased by the said Mount Vernon Ladies Association of the Union shall be forever held by it sacred to the father of his country; and if from any cause the said association shall cease to exist, the property owned by the said association shall revert to the commonwealth of Virginia, sacred to the purposes for which it was originally purchased."

2. This act shall be in force from its passage.

And on the 6th day of April, 1858, Mrs. Ann Pamelia Cunningham, Southern

Matron, Regent, on behalf of the Association, entered into an agreement with John A. Washington for the purchase of Mount Vernon, or at least, that part now held by them (the original tract contained 4,000 acres), conditioned for the payment of $18,000 in cash; one bond of the said Association for $57,000, payable 1st January, 1859; one other bond of said Association for $41,666.66, payable 22d February, 1860; one other bond of said Association for $41,666.67, payable on 22d February, 1861; and one other bond of said Association for $41,666.67, payable on 22d February, 1862, with lawful interest on each of the bonds from their dates. "And retaining in him the said John Augustine Washington, his heirs and assigns, the title to the property aforesaid, with the possession thereof, until the sum of two hundred thousand dollars, with all the interest which may accrue as hereinafter mentioned, shall have been fully paid to him or them." * (This condition appears in the said agreement before the dates and amounts of the bonds are inserted.)

A short time prior to the breaking out of the late war, the Association effected an arrangement by which they were enabled to discharge the entire amount of their indebtedness and to cancel all their bonds; but it appears upon an examination of the Records of Fairfax county, that they have not, as yet, obtained a title deed for their property.

The Agent of the Association is Mr. Upton H. Herbert, who, though having many near relatives and friends in the army of the late Confederate States, yet remained faithful to his post, still resides at Mt. Vernon and superintends the care of the place. It was the object of the Association to improve the lands by all those attractions of art which add so much to the charms of natural advantages, but the late war has very materially interfered with this design. The politeness and attention of Mr. Herbert to visitors leaves nothing unenjoyed by them which they could expect.

Note 3, Page 1.—"EVERY PAGE." It will be observed that this resolution was overlooked at page 23, probably from the word Washington (the city) having been the last word on the page and mistaken for his own name.

Note 4, Page 1.—"LAST WILL AND TESTAMENT." The last Will and Testament of George Washington, admitted to probate and executed as such, was written, as will be seen by its perusal, in the summer of 1799, and dated the 9th day of July of that year, but a few months prior to his death. It will be found singularly complete and minute in its description and disposition of his immense estate, and these facts are but in keeping with the traits that marked every act, and effort of his wonderful career. As he was always ready in time for every duty of his life, so he would seem to have finished just in time the last worldly preparation for death—for in spiritual readiness he had been long prepared, and having "set his house in order," there was nothing to shackle his spirit in the last struggle with the great Conqueror. As the last will and testament of the Father of his Country is of peculiar interest to all who cherish his memory, we have deemed it important that a short history of it should be here inserted. As we have before stated, it was written in the summer of 1799, and dated the 9th day of July, and it would seem the testator omitted the word "nine" after "seventeen hundred and ninety" in dating his will; however, it is very certain it was intended to have been so written, as he finishes the sentence thus: "and of the Independence of the United States the twenty-fourth."

On the morning of the 14th December, 1799, between ten and eleven o'clock, he departed this life. "A few moments before he expired," writes Mr. Lear,† "he made several efforts to speak. At length he said, 'I am just going. Have me decently buried, and do not let my body be put in the vault in less than

* The entire agreement is recorded in Liber A, No. 4, folios 19, &c., of Fairfax County Land Records.

† Mr. Tobias Lear, of New Hampshire, a graduate of Harvard College Mr. L. had been in the family from about 1785, as private secretary to Washington, and in charge of the instruction of G. W. P. and Miss Nellie Custis — Washington's adopted children.

three days after I am dead.' He then looked at me again and said, 'Do you understand me?' I replied, 'Yes.' "'Tis well,' said he." These were the last words that passed the lips of the great Christian, soldier and statesman. His funeral took place at Mount Vernon, December 18, 1799, without that pomp and parade that usually attends the obsequies of great generals or statesmen. The Rev. Mr. Davis read the funeral service at the vault, and pronounced a short but affecting address; after which the Masons, to which order he had been attached many years, performed their solemn ceremonies, and the body was deposited in the vault. At a Court held for the County of Fairfax on the 20th day of January, 1800, the will (of which this is a copy) was presented in open court by *George Steptoe Washington, Samuel Washington* and *Lawrence Lewis*, three of the executors mentioned in said will; and they making oath thereto, and the same being proved by the oaths of Charles Little, Charles Simms and Ludwell Lee, to be in the true handwriting of the testator, as also the Schedule and Notes thereto attached, on motion the same were ordered to be *recorded*,* " and a certificate was granted said executors for obtaining probat thereof in due form."

This order was taken by the County Court of Fairfax, Virginia, and entered up by George Deneale, then Clerk of said Court.† As Fairfax County contains Mount Vernon and the remains of our loved Washington, we deem it pertinent and as a matter of general interest, to give in brief the general outlines of its formation and other matter connected with its history. It was in 1741 a part of Prince William County, but in 1742, by an act of the Virginia Assembly, Fairfax was created a separate county, with the Potomac river as its northern and eastern boundary, Bull Run, as its southern boundary, and Loudoun County as its western boundary; and in the fall and winter of the same year (1742) an organization of the County was completed, with its Courts, &c. Catesby Cooke, Gent., was the first Clerk of the Court, whose commission was given by John Robinson, Secretary of the Colony of Virginia under the reign of George II., at Williamsburg, December —, 1742, and qualified as such —— December, 1742, and *was recorded*‡ in Liber A, No. 1, folios 1 and 2, of said County records. After the death of Catesby Cooke, which occurred in 1746, John Graham was by Thomas Nelson, under authority from William Adair, then Secretary of said Colony, appointed to succeed him, by commission dated at Williamsburg, December 9, 1746. After this period, the power being vested in the Court to choose their Clerk, we find Peter Waggener to have succeeded John Graham, by a record of 17th October, 1752. Mr. Waggener remained Clerk of said County until his decease, which occurred in 1798, when we find by records of May 21, 1798, George Deneale, Esq., to have been appointed Clerk, being the fourth since the organization of said County, before whom the Executors of the last will and testament of George Washington qualified. Subsequent to this period, the County was, by an act of the Virginia Assembly, extended, taking a portion from Loudoun County, making Sugar-Land Run the western boundary and dividing line between that portion of Fairfax and Loudoun. In 1800 the Virginia Assembly ceded that portion of Fairfax, which is now known as Alexandria County, to the general Government, to comprise that portion of the District of Columbia on the south side of the Potomac which was afterwards retroceded to the State of Virginia, and is now known as Alexandria County. Bleeding at every pore where once vitality and active life existed, it is her pride to boast of scions of Virginia's best blood—men in whose veins course the blood of *Washington*, the *Lees*, the *Masons*, *Fairfaxes*, and many other old and time-honored families whose members have been *Virginia's* and their *country's*

---

* Recorded in Liber H, No. 1, folios 1, 2, &c., of the Records of Fairfax County, Virginia.

† See copy of Order after Washington's Notes.

‡ The sheet containing folios 1 and 2 was torn from Liber A by Federal soldiers while Fairfax C. H. was occupied by them during the late war. The original manuscript on which the commission was written, with the signature of the Secretary of the Colony, (John Robinson,) and *Seal* of said Colony, is now in possession of the Publisher of this volume.

brightest ornaments as soldiers, statesmen, and jurists, and who, as their fathers did, "always keep the latch-string out to both stranger and friend."

In 1853, Alfred Moss (now deceased), then Clerk of the County Court of said County, asked the Legislature of Virginia the privilege of withdrawing the original will of General George Washington from the County Records for the purpose of having it lithographed, and on the 22d March, 1853, the following Act was passed :

"1. Be it enacted by the general assembly, that Alfred Moss, the Clerk of the County Court of Fairfax, be and he is hereby authorized, under the direction, and with the permission of the County Court of Fairfax, to withdraw from the Records of the County Court of Fairfax the original Will of General George Washington, and to carry the same beyond the limits of the Commonwealth, and to entrust the same to the custody of an engraver, to be selected by him for the purpose of having said original will lithographed ; provided however, that the said Alfred Moss shall, before removing the said will, satisfy the said County Court of Fairfax, that he has taken the necessary steps to insure the safe keeping of the said will while in the hands of the engraver, and to cause the same to be restored to the files of the County Court, after the same shall be lithographed.

"2. This Act shall be in force from its passage."

And afterwards, the said Court having given their consent to the same, Mr. Moss endeavored to have the will lithographed, but from causes unknown, he never accomplished his purpose, and until now the will has never been published. Washington Irving, in his life of Washington, publishes only a part of it ; and we find upon comparing his publication with the *original*, that the *portion* he gives as taken from it, is entirely incorrect.* In July, 1861, when the Confederate army fell back from Fairfax C. H., Mr. Moss *carefully enveloped* Washington's will, endorsing thereon ;

" The Original Will of
GENERAL GEORGE WASHINGTON.

Belongs to the Records of Fairfax County Court. To be returned to me, or any one legally authorized to receive it.

ALFRED MOSS, CLERK,
Fairfax County Court."

The will, with other Records of his Court, was then carried to Richmond Virginia, and the will deposited with George W. Mumford, Esq., then Secretary of the Commonwealth of Virginia. In 1862, Henry T. Brooks, who had been elected to fill the Clerkship thus vacated by Alfred Moss, published over his signature, an article, which was copied in many of the papers of the Northern press, stating that Mr. Moss "had taken away the will of General Washington, and that it had been *sold*, and was then on exhibition in the *British Museum.*" As both of these gentlemen died before the close of the late war, we would say, in *justice* to them, that Mr. Brooks had been *imposed* upon by some one, or had been badly *informed* as to its whereabouts, and that great *injustice* was done Mr. Moss. Mr. Moss having died in the fall of 1862, Mr. Thomas Moore, his deputy, was appointed in the following spring, Clerk, *pro tempore,* of said Court. In a conversation with Mr. Moore, he remarked that in the spring of 1863, he, as said Clerk, called upon Mr. Mumford, who assured him of the safety and preservation of the will. He permitted it to continue with the Secretary of the State, where it remained until the summer of 1865, when Mr. O. W. Huntt, who had been selected by the County Court of said County to look up the missing records and papers of their Court, received it from Mr. Lewis, then occupying the position formerly held by Mr. Mumford, who stated that the will had been found in his office among the papers lying scattered by Federal soldiers, on the floor of one of the rooms. Mr. Huntt returned the will, with other records, &c., to the County, where it is now on file in charge of Ferdinand D. Richard-

---

* *Vide* Irving's Life of Washington, V., folio 358.

son, the present Clerk of said Court; and though from frequent handling has been considerably torn, and can only be deciphered with the greatest patience, and by comparing with the record heretofore referred to, yet is eagerly sought for and read by those visiting Fairfax C. H. In consideration of its condition, the Court at its November Term, 1865, passed the following order:

"It appearing to the Court that the original will of General George Washington, of Mount Vernon, has been much worn and mutilated from frequent handling, and that it is liable to further injury from the same cause; it is ordered that the Clerk of this Court purchase, at the expense of the County, a suitable case, in which he is directed to deposit the said will."

This order was not carried into effect by Mr. William H. Fitzhugh, then Clerk, from what cause we did not learn, but were informed by Mr. Richardson that it was his intention to carry out the order as soon as he could have a suitable case constructed, which is to be of glass, that parties visiting his office in search of it may look upon, without handling it.

Note 5, Page 1.—"MARTHA WASHINGTON." General Washington first met her in 1758 at Mr. Chamberlayne's, near the Pamunky, a branch of the York river, while he was on his way from Winchester to Williamsburg to lay before the military council there assembled the destitute condition of the Virginia troops. At this time, says Irving, "she was a young and blooming widow, Mrs. Martha Custis, daughter of John Dandridge, both patrician names in the provinces." Her husband, John Parke Custis, had been dead about three years, leaving her with two young children.* She is represented as being rather small in stature, but extremely well formed, with a pleasant countenance, dark hazel eyes and hair, with those frank, engaging manners so peculiar to and captivating in Southern ladies. Added to these attractions, she was possessed of a large fortune. It seems that though Washington was on urgent business, requiring immediate attention, he for once deviated from his usual *prompt attention* to business entrusted to his care, and instead of leaving Mr. Chamberlayne's that evening, as contemplated, orders for the horses were countermanded, and it was not until next morning that he was again in the saddle, for Williamsburg.

The *White House*,† the residence of Mrs. Custis, was in New Kent County, but a short distance from that city. So he had frequent opportunities to visit the beautiful and fascinating young widow; and we have no doubt that while at Williamsburg he had both engaged her affection and hand, for we are told by Irving,‡ that immediately after the reduction of Fort Duquesne,§ and the French domination of the Ohio being at an end, and quiet once more restored to his native province, he retired from the service. His marriage with Mrs. Custis took place shortly after his return. It was celebrated on the 6th of January, 1759, at the White House, the residence of the bride, in the good old hospitable style of Virginia, amid a joyous assemblage of relatives and friends.

Note 6, Page 2.—"SHALL RECEIVE THEIR FREEDOM." "From private letters which we have been kindly permitted to peruse, and from many expressions used by him in his will, it seems that it had long been his earnest wish to emancipate the slaves held by him *in his own right;*" but from causes that appear manifest in the perusal of his will, and show his great forethought and kind consideration of them, it was impracticable and grating to the kind feelings of his good and generous heart. But when we consider that after providing for the loved one whom God had given him as a companion for earth's pilgrimage, the first object that engaged his attention was his loving and faithful slaves, we must at once see of how great magnitude this great and good Southern soldier, statesman and patriot considered this great moral evil, slavery, though born and

---

* John Parke Custis and his sister. This young lady died at Mount Vernon, in the 17th year of her age, on the 19th of June, 1773.

† From which the President's mansion in Washington derived its name.

‡ Irving's Life of Washington, Vol. 1, 264.   § Now Pittsburg.

educated a slaveholder. In a letter to John F. Mercer, of Virginia, in September, 1786, he writes: "I never mean, unless some particular circumstances should compel me to it, to possess another slave by purchase, it being among my *first* wishes to see some plan adopted by which slavery in this country may be abolished by law." *

"And eleven years afterwards, in August, 1797, he writes to his nephew, Lawrence Lewis, which we have had in our hands, "I wish from my soul that the legislature of this State could see the policy of a gradual abolition of slavery. It might prevent much future mischief." † How prophetic! Had one been inspired by the Almighty he could not have spoken with more truth. He saw that sectional hatred being engendered and nurtured on its account which burst upon our once happy country in 1860–61 like some destroying angel of the avenging gods. Washington was not alone in his views upon this subject. Jefferson and many other prominent men of their day were of the same opinion; and had not fanaticism, blind fanaticism, been turned loose to prey upon reason, all that has been accomplished at the expense of millions and millions of treasure, with a national blackness of mourning shrouding every hearthstone throughout the length and breadth of our desolated land, might have been, ere the close of the present generation, effected peaceably and quietly, leaving a united, harmonious and prosperous people, without national *cemeteries* for martyrs to principle, without a Booth or an assassinated President to mark the annals of our country's history.

Note 7, Page 2.—"DOWER NEGROES." These negroes he only had a life interest in by his marriage with Mrs. Custis, and at her death, as a matter of course, went to heirs of her husband, John Parke Custis; hence he says, "it not being in my power under the tenure by which the dower negroes are held to manumit them." Mrs. Martha Washington, in 1801, manumitted all the slaves she held in her own right. This deed of manumission was recorded in Liber C. C., folio 323, of Fairfax County Records, and lost during the war, therefore we cannot arrive at the number thus liberated.

Note 8, Page 2.—"SUPPORT THEMSELVES." We find that there were many of this class, and were a heavy expense, supported by the Executors out of the proceeds of his estate for numbers of years; as late as the year 1832, when the last estate account of Washington was settled by John A. Washington, Executor of Bushrod Washington, the last surviving executor of the will, we find the estate charged as having paid out for rent, clothing, provisions, coffins and funeral expenses, the sum of $788.05. The last item of these charges being for funeral expenses of *three free negroes*, $12.00, dated December 31, 1829.‡

Note 9, Page 3.—"TO READ AND WRITE." This provision of the will was never carried into effect, as the statutory laws of the State of Virginia expressly prohibited schools for the instruction of negroes.

Note 10, Page 4.—"WILLIAM" (calling himself William Lee) was the body servant and constant attendant of Washington during the Revolutionary war, and until his injuries incapacitated him for the position. After this, Christopher became his favorite servant, and attended him with that fidelity, affectionate watchfulness and anxiety that has ever been the marked characteristic of the Southern slave when kindly treated and well cared for. William has become quite famous, having had as many as five different funerals, and each claiming to be that of the original William: once he died in North Carolina, once in Missouri, and once in Arkansas; and we are of opinion that we have seen two

* Irving's Washington, V, folio 288.
† Irving's Washington, Vol. 5, folio 299.
‡ Will Book Q, folio 262, Fairfax County Records.

accounts stating that the original William had died at different times in New York ; the last time occurring in the winter of 1867. The William, of whom in all probability these accounts are but mere fabrications, most likely died at his master's old homestead, Mount Vernon.

Note 11, Page 4.—"ALEXANDRIA ACADEMY." The corner stone of this institution was laid on the 7th of September, 1785, by the Alexandria Lodge (No. 39) of Free Masons, of which lodge Washington was a member : he was also a patron and one of the Trustees of the Academy. The building was erected and is yet standing on the lot at the corner of Washington and Wolfe Streets. The late Dr. Elias Harrison, of Alexandria, Virginia, was one of the Professors in the days of its prosperity. Many of the students of this institution became eminent men, amongst whom were General R. E. Lee, the late Senator Pearce, of Maryland, and others. The old Academy building in the course of time became private property ; and the corporate authorities of Alexandria assumed the Trusteeship of the Washington endowment, and built a larger structure for the accommodation of a greater number of pupils, and the name changed from "Alexandria Academy" to that of " Washington School." Col. S. King Shay, an old and respected citizen of Alexandria, is now its principal, and at different times in charge eighteen years, once for sixteen consecutive years.

Note 12, Page 6.—For many years Washington had been convinced of the practicability of an easy and short communication between the Potomac and James rivers and the waters of the Ohio, thence to the great chain of northern lakes, and saw plainly the immense advantages that must finally accrue to his native State, Virginia, and had gone so far as to attempt the organization of a company to undertake at their own expense the opening of such communication, but the breaking out of the American Revolution put a stop to the enterprise. In 1784, in company with Dr. Craik, he visited the waters of the Ohio, Kanawha, and other western waters of his State, to make observations and collect information on the subject. After his return, upon his suggesting the opening of said communication, Benjamin Harrison, the Governor of Virginia, being struck with his ideas of the plan for opening the navigation of the western waters, laid the matter before the State Legislature. Washington immediately repaired to Richmond. He arrived there on the 15th day of November, 1784, and in the latter part of December of the same year, we find him at Annapolis, at the request of the Virginia Assembly, arranging matters with the Assembly of Maryland, respecting the communication between the Potomac and western waters. Through his individual exertions and influence, two companies were formed under the fostering care of these States, for opening the navigation of the Potomac and James rivers, and he was immediately appointed president of both.

By a unanimous vote of the Virginia Assembly, in 1785, fifty shares in the Potomac and one hundred shares in the James River company were appropriated for his benefit. The aggregate amount of these shares was about $40,000. This seems greatly to have embarrassed him, as the reader will perceive. He at first declined, but subsequently accepted the shares, upon condition that he should be permitted to appropriate them to public uses, which condition the Virginia Legislature accepted. Thus, to our loved Washington, do we owe the vast and incalculable benefits derived from these great inland water communications.

Note 13, Page 9.—"UNIVERSITY." In his message to Congress, convened January 8, 1790, he says that furnishing the means of higher education at the seat of government was "well worthy of a place in the deliberations of the Legislature." Seven years later, in 1797, in his last appeal to Congress on the subject, he says of the assimilation of the principles, opinions and manners of our countrymen, by the common education of a portion of our youth from every quarter, that "the more homogeneous our citizens can be made in these particulars, the greater will be the prospect of a permanent union." It seems this coveted desire was never carried into effect, and the fifty shares thus donated reverted to the estate.

Note 14, Page 10.—"LIBERTY HALL ACADEMY," now WASHINGTON COLLEGE, had its origin in a classical school established before the war of American Independence, by the early settlers of the Valley of Virginia.

During the period of its infancy, it was sustained by the munificence of its founders, who secured for it in 1782 its present charter, the school bearing the name of LIBERTY HALL ACADEMY until 1798, when it was styled WASHINGTON ACADEMY, in honor of its great benefactor, and subsequently WASHINGTON COLLEGE.

The Virginia Legislature, attesting their appreciation of the unexampled merits of GEORGE WASHINGTON, in October, 1784, passed an act vesting in him one hundred shares in the James River Navigation Company, which he declined, except on condition that the Legislature would permit him to transfer the donation to some object of a a public nature. In compliance with the wishes of Gen. WASHINGTON, the Legislature substituted for the act of October, 1784, an act of October, 1785, providing that this fund be conveyed to him to be applied as he might indicate. Gen. WASHINGTON determined to appropriate this gift of Virginia to the endowment of an institution of learning upon the upper waters of James river, and accordingly, by his will, conveyed it to LIBERTY HALL ACADEMY. This munificent endowment now yields to the College the interest upon $50,000 annually.

Subsequently the CINCINNATI SOCIETY, an organization composed of Revolutionary Officers and having for its object the relief of indigent persons of this class, after accomplishing the purposes for which they organized, determined to convey the funds in their treasury to some public institution, and influenced, as they avowed, by the example of Gen. WASHINGTON, bestowed the gift upon WASHINGTON COLLEGE. From this donation the College now enjoys an endowment of $23,000.

In 1826, JOHN ROBINSON, of Rockbridge County, Virginia, a revolutionary soldier, bequeathed to the same object his estate, which yielded about $40,000, and enabled the Trustees to increase very materially the philosophical apparatus and the buildings of the College. In acknowledgment of this generous bequest the "*Robinson Professorship of Physical Science*" was established.

Thus thrice endowed so liberally by revolutionary heroes, WASHINGTON COLLEGE became a seat of learning to which were attracted many young men of Virginia and other States, whose influence became conspicuous in the pulpit, the forum, and the halls of legislation—among whom may be named the ALEXANDERS, the STUARTS, the McDOWELLS, the PRESTONS, and many others that fill an enviable place in the history of our country.

In the Spring of 1861, the College was enjoying a full share of public patronage, but its regular exercises were interrupted, and for a time suspended altogether. The students, animated by the spirit that moved the young men of the South generally, organized themselves into a military company, joined the immortal JACKSON at Winchester, and for four years shared the fortunes of the STONEWALL BRIGADE, winning from their illustrious commander the designation of "*more than brave young men.*" Many of them do not survive to witness the present prosperity of their Alma Mater.

In the month of June, 1864, Gen. DAVID HUNTER occupied the town of Lexington, and under his eyes the College that bore the name and enjoyed the munificence of GEORGE WASHINGTON, was sacked; its chemical and philosophical apparatus destroyed; and its *libraries*, to a great extent, ruined.

The Board of Trustees, at a meeting held in the summer of 1865, took steps to repair these desolations, in which they have been, to a gratifying extent, successful; and in order to establish the Institution on a firmer footing than it ever before held, upon the acceptance of the Presidency by General R. E. LEE, they resolved to expand the sphere of its operations, and, by an enlarged scientific course, to give it a place among the first institutions of the land, thus responding emphatically to the material wants of the country.

Mr. C. H. McCormick, a Virginian, born and reared in the vicinity of Washington College and now a wealthy citizen of New York, bestowed the generous gift of $15,000, by which the Trustees have been enabled to establish the "*McCormick Professorship of Experimental Philosophy and Practical Mechanics.*"

The late Mr. Warren Newcomb, of New York City, made the liberal donation of $10,000, and thus rendered essential aid in filling other chairs.

Mr. Rathmell Wilson, of Philadelphia, desiring to repair the damage done the College Library by the troops under command of Gen. David Hunter, donated a large number of rare and valuable books belonging to the library of his brother, the late Thomas B. Wilson, whose name is conspicuously associated with the Academy of Natural Sciences, and the Entomological Society of Philadelphia.

From a Catalogue for 1867, kindly furnished the publisher by the President, General R. E. Lee, we find the number of students to have been 399, now probably far exceeding 400.

Note 15, Page 11.—That generous fatherly affection and charity which had ever marked his treatment of and liberality toward relatives, is here prominently displayed in providing for the transfer of this property in question, since none of the parties had legal titles thereto.

Note 16, Page 13.—This provision of his will was strictly and religiously carried into effect. It would seem that Bartholomew Dandridge left his estate considerably involved, and to liberate so large a number of the working force on the plantation of his widow immediately, would have created great distress to her and her children, and would have turned upon the charity of the County or State many old and decrepid, as well as young and helpless slaves, unable to shift for themselves : hence this wise provision.

Note 17, Page 14.—"Bushrod Washington," son of John A. Washington, third brother by his father's last marriage, and the father of Col. John Augustine, late proprietor of Mount Vernon. To him and his son Col. John A. Washington, do we owe the preservation of all the valuable papers and relics of our loved Washington ; many of which are at present in possession of the family of the late Col. John A. Washington, who resides near Charlestown, Jefferson Co., West Virginia.

Note 18, Page 15.—"Gt. Kanhawa." We find in many of the writings, both historical and private, the Kanawha thus spelt, and we have no doubt that it is the proper spelling of the Indian name from which it was taken. The pronunciation would remain the same.

Note 19, Page 15.—"In the County of Loudoun." This is clearly an error, as the County of Loudoun never embraced that portion of Fairfax. This tract is situated on Difficult run, near where it crosses the Pike leading from George Town to Leesburg, Virginia, and was sold by Washington's executors to the Sheppards, of Fairfax, and is now owned by Mr. Thomas Peacock, of said County.

Note 20, Page 17.—"Lawrence and Robert Washington." We are not advised as to whether or not any relationship existed between them and the testator, but from this clause, and no evidence that any did, we are inclined to the belief they were, as he says, "acquaintances and friends of my juvenile years."

Note 21, Page 17.—"Dr. Craik." Dr. James Craik, a gentleman who probably enjoyed as much if not more of Washington's confidence and esteem than any other man, and who attended him in his last illness,* was a young Scotchman, well bred, and of superior mind and attainments. He, like Dr. Hugh Mercer, of Revolutionary fame, fled from Scotland after the defeat of Charles Edward, at Culloden, and settled in the Colony of Virginia. He was commissioned on the same day that Washington was, as an officer in the war against the French and Indians ; and we find him with Washington at Great Meadows in May, 1754, as Surgeon of a Virginia Regiment, and during the continuance of this war we find him intimately connected with him. Again we find him, in 1777, with Washington. "About this time, (May, 1777,) Washington had the satisfaction of drawing near him his old friend and travelling companion, Dr. James Craik, the same who had served with him in Braddock's campaign, and had voyaged with him down the Ohio ; for whom he now procured the appointment of assistant director-general of the Hospital department of the middle district, which included the States between the Hudson and the Potomac. In offering the situation to the doctor, he writes : ' You know how far you may be benefited or injured by such an appointment, and whether it is advisable or practicable for you to quit your family and practice at this time. I request, as a friend, that my proposing this matter to you may have no influence upon your acceptance of it. I have no other end in view than to serve you.' "* This position he filled to the entire satisfaction of his friends and with great credit to himself. After the termination of the Revolution, he located in Alexandria, Virginia, where he continued the practice of his profession until his death. He continued through life the attached and devoted friend of Washington.†

Note 22, Page 17.—"REV. NOW BRYAN LORD FAIRFAX," was brother of George Wm. Fairfax, and son of old Lord Fairfax, of Belvoir notoriety, but who, at the breaking out of the Revolutionary war, and for some time prior (1752 or 3,) resided at Greenway Court, near Winchester. Lord Fairfax was a great admirer of Washington's military genius, as well as his great moral worth and intelligence. During the French war we find that he was frequently in Washington's camp, near Winchester, aiding the young commander with his counsels or his sword. Washington had been from his early youth warmly attached to the Fairfaxes ; owing, probably, in part to the intimacy which existed between him and them,— his brother, Lawrence Washington, having married the daughter of the Hon. William Fairfax, of Fairfax County — and his frequent visits to Belvoir. When Washington presided as moderator of a public meeting, held by the inhabitants of Fairfax County to discuss the recent acts of the British Parliament, and was appointed chairman of a committee to draw up resolutions expressive of the sentiments of that meeting, and to report the same to a general meeting of the County, to be held at the Court House on the 18th of July, 1774, he saw, and with painful emotions, that "the course that public measures were taking, shocked the loyal feelings of his valued friend, Bryan Fairfax." ‡ When the news of Lexington reached Mount Vernon, Bryan Fairfax was Washington's guest. Irving says, "The worthy and gentle-spirited Fairfax deplored it deeply." He saw too plainly that all his pleasant relations in life must be broken up and his dearest friends arrayed against the government to which he was loyally attached and had determined to adhere. This had rendered his situation among his former friends embarrassing and unpleasant, and while he disapproved of the measures of the British government which had severed the colonies from England, yet he was, as we have above intimated, loyal to his king. He therefore determined to go to England and remain until peace should be restored to his loved colony, Virginia. To effect this purpose he visited Washington, at that time with the army at Valley Forge. Washington, who knew his feelings best, and respected his conscientiousness, we are told, received him with that warm cordiality of former and happier days, for with him he brought recollections dearest to his heart, of Mount Vernon and Belvoir, happy days of invigorating pleasures on the beautiful banks of Virginia's noble old Potomac. As it was Mr. Fairfax's intention to embark at New York,

* See Irving's Washington, Vol. v, folio 294, &c.
† Irving's Washington, Vol. iii, folio 68.
‡ Irving's Washington, Vol. I, folio 354.

Washington furnished him with the necessary papers to insure his safety to that city. After arriving there, the conscience of Mr. Fairfax would not permit him to take the oaths required to secure his passage to England; he therefore obtained permission from the British commander to return to his home in Virginia, where he continued to reside until his death, which happened in 1802, at seventy-five years of age. He became proprietor of Belvoir, and after the death of his father, heir to the family title, but the latter he never assumed. In the latter part of his life he became a clergyman of the Episcopal Church. Old Lord Fairfax, of Greenway Court, Washington's early friend and patron, lived to an aged man at his beautiful retreat in the Shenandoah, and at his death had attained his ninety-second year. The reverend historiographer of Mount Vernon records his death in homely prose and verse, thus:

"When old Lord Fairfax heard that Washington had captured Lord Cornwallis and all his army, he called to his black waiter, 'Come, Joe! carry me to bed, for it is high time for me to die!

> Then up rose Joe, all at the word,
> And took his master's arm,
> And thus to bed he softly led
> The lord of Greenway farm.
>
> There oft he called on Britain's name,
> And oft he wept full sore,
> Then sighed—thy will, oh Lord, be done—
> And word spake never more."

[See Weems' *Life of Washington*.

Though frank and open in his adherence to Great Britain, he lived unmolested by the Whigs, and was popular and highly respected by his neighbors.

Note 23, Page 17.—"GEN. DE LA FAYETTE," whose memory will be embalmed for all time in the American heart by reason of his aid in our struggle for liberty from the tyranny of Great Britain.

Note 24, Page 18.—"TOBIAS LEAR." Washington had long had him in his service as private secretary and preceptor to his adopted children, George Washington Parke Custis and sister.

Note 25, Page 21.—These two gentlemen were sons of Lund Washington, who, though bearing the same name, and as has been said, of the same stock, does not appear to have been in any near degree of relationship. He was for years manager of Washington's Mount Vernon estate, during the American revolution, and it was to him that he wrote from the American camp at Cambridge, in 1775, a short time before he was joined by his family, the celebrated letter in regard to the hospitality of Mount Vernon, which we here insert. Says he: "Let the hospitality of the house with respect to the poor be kept up. Let no one go hungry away. If any of this kind of people should be in want of corn, supply their necessaries; provided it does not encourage them to idleness; and I have no objection to your giving my money in charity to the amount of forty or fifty pounds a year, when you think it well bestowed. What I mean by having no objection is, that it is my desire it should be done. You are to consider that neither *myself nor wife is* now in the way to do these good offices."

Note 26, Page 22.—"ELEANOR PARKE CUSTIS AND GEORGE WASHINGTON PARKE CUSTIS." These were the children of John Parke Custis, the only child of Mrs. Washington by her first husband, Mr. John Parke Custis, that lived to its majority. They were, when very young, adopted by Washington.

Note 27, Page 23.—This is the tract now known as "Arlington," which the late war has made historic, as "Arlington Heights." After the death of George W. P. Custis it descended to General Robert E. Lee, who had married the daughter of Mr. Custis, and is now held by the United States as confiscated property, and used as a National Cemetery for Union Soldiers and home for *Freedmen.*

Note 28, Page 27.—This was done not long after his death, and is the one in which his remains, with others of his family, are deposited.

Note 29, Page 28.—From a careful examination of Records, and after having made diligent enquiry, we can safely say that, though so large and valuable an estate was distributed among so many legatees, yet not one dispute sufficient to cause litigation ever arose,

www.ingramcontent.com/pod-product-compliance
Lightning Source LLC
Chambersburg PA
CBHW022023080426
42733CB00007B/697